Christmas Sheet Music

For Cello

Table of Contents

Table of Contents²

Cello

1. Angels From The Realms of Glory

James Montgomery

Arrangement & Transcription by Willy Espinoza

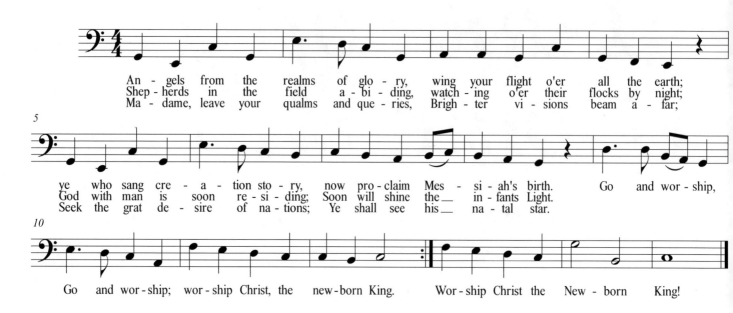

An - gels from the realms of glo - ry, wing your flight o'er all the earth;
Shep - herds in the field a - bi - ding, watch - ing o'er their flocks by night;
Ma - dame, leave your qualms and que - ries, Brigh - ter vi - sions beam a - far;

ye who sang cre - a - tion sto - ry, now pro - claim Mes - si - ah's birth.   Go and wor - ship,
God with man is soon re - si - ding; Soon will shine the__ in - fants Light.
Seek the grat de - sire of na - tions; Ye shall see his__ na - tal star.

Go and wor - ship; wor - ship Christ, the new - born King.   Wor - ship Christ the New - born King!

Cello

2. Angels We Have Heard On High

Traditional French Song

Arrangement & Transcription by Willy Espinoza

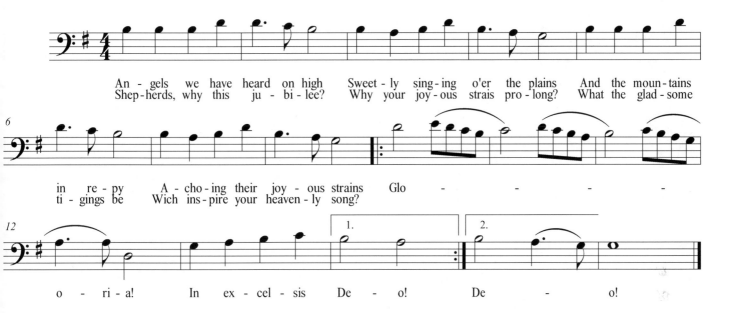

An - gels   we have   heard on high   Sweet - ly   sing - ing   o'er   the plains   And   the moun - tains
Shep - herds, why this   ju - bi - lee?   Why your   joy - ous   strais pro - long?   What   the glad - some

in   re - py   A - cho - ing   their   joy - ous strains   Glo   -   -   -   -
ti - gings be   Wich   ins - pire your heaven - ly song?

o   -   ri - a!   In   ex - cel - sis   De - o!   De   -   o!

2

3. As with Gladness Men of Old

William Chatterton Dix

Arrangement & Transcription by Willy Espinoza

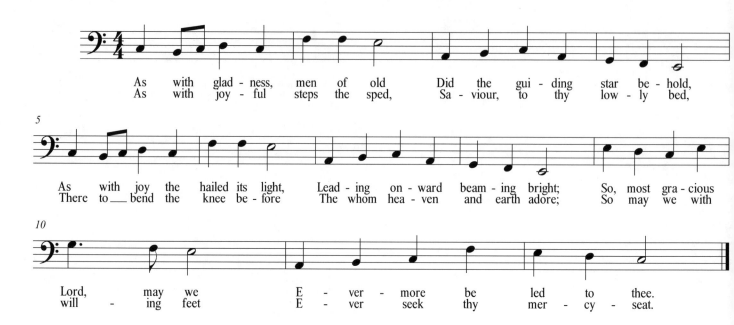

As with glad - ness, men of old Did the gui - ding star be - hold,
As with joy - ful steps the sped, Sa - viour, to thy low - ly bed,

As with joy the hailed its light, Lead - ing on - ward beam - ing bright; So, most gra - cious
There to bend the knee be - fore The whom hea - ven and earth adore; So may we with

Lord, may we E - ver - more be led to thee.
will - ing feet E - ver seek thy mer - cy - seat.

4. Auld Lang Syne

Doguie McLean

Arrangement & Transcription by Willy Espinoza

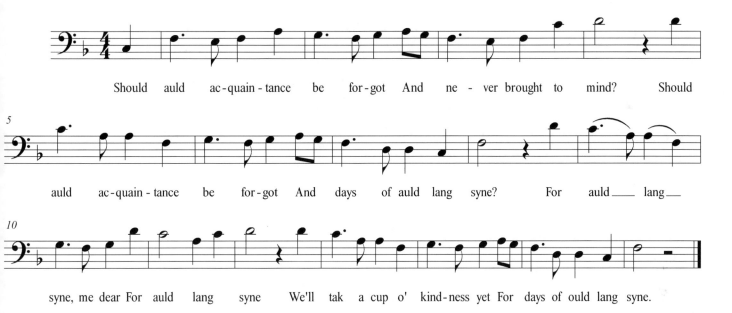

Should auld ac-quain-tance be for-got And ne-ver brought to mind? Should

auld ac-quain-tance be for-got And days of auld lang syne? For auld___ lang___

syne, me dear For auld lang syne We'll tak a cup o' kind-ness yet For days of ould lang syne.

4

5. Away in a Manger

Arrangement & Transcription by Willy Espinoza

A way in a— man - ger No— crib for a bed The lit - tle Lord Je - sus La - id
stars in the bright sky Looked down where He lay As -

down His sweet Head The
- - - - - -
sleep on the hay.

6. Bring a Torch, Jeanette Isabella

Loreena McKennitt

Arrangement & Transcription by Willy Espinoza

Bring   a   torch,____   Jea - nette I - sa - bel - la   Bring   a   torch, to   the   cra - dle run!
It   is   wrong when the   Child is   s - leep - ing   It   is   wrong____ to   talk   so   loud;

It   is   je - sus, good folk   of   the   vil - lage   Christ   is   born   and   Ma - ry's cal - ling Ah!   ah!
Si - lence, all,   as   you   ga - ther   a - round,____   Lest____ your noise should   wa - ken Je - sus: Hush!   hush!

beau - ti - ful   is   the   mo - ther!   Ah!   ah!   beau - ti - ful is   her   Son!
see____ how fast   He   slum - bers: Hush!   hush!   see____ how fast   He   sleeps!

6

7. Christ Was Born On Christmas Day

Arrangement & Transcription by Willy Espinoza

When Christ was born,   On Christ-mas Day   When Christ was born on Christ-mas
Oh when we hear,   The Christ-mas Bells,   Oh when we hear the Christ-mas

Day   Oh how I want to be that num-ber,   When we hear the Christ-mas Bells.
Bells.

8. Come, Thou Long-Expected Jesus

Arrangement & Transcription by Willy Espinoza

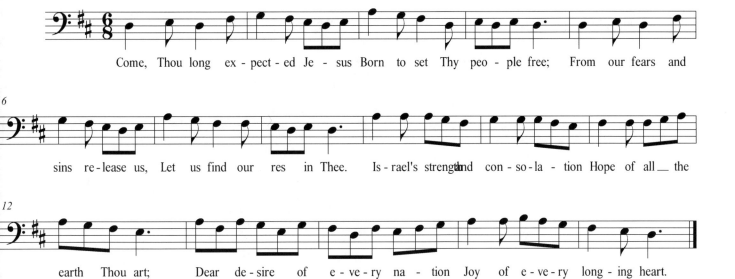

Come, Thou long ex-pect-ed Je - sus Born to set Thy peo - ple free; From our fears and

sins re-lease us, Let us find our res in Thee. Is-rael's strength and con-so-la - tion Hope of all __ the

earth Thou art; Dear de - sire of e - ve-ry na - tion Joy of e - ve - ry long - ing heart.

9. The Coventry Carol

Traditional

Arrangement & Transcription by Willy Espinoza

Lul - ly, lul - la, thou lit - tle ti-ny child, Ba - by, ul - ly lul - lay, thou

lit - tle ti - ny child, Ba - by, lul - ly lul - lay.

10. Deck The Halls

Traditional
Arrangement & Transcription by Willy Espinoza

Deck the halls with boughs of hol - ly   fa la la la la   la   la la la   Don we now our
'Tis the sea - sons to   be jol - ly

gay ap - pa - rel   Fa la la   la la la   la   la la   Troll   the an - cient

Yule - tide ca - rol   Fa la la la la   la   la la la   la.

11. Ding, Dong Merrily on High

Traditional / Andy Quin
Arrangement & Transcription by Willy Espinoza

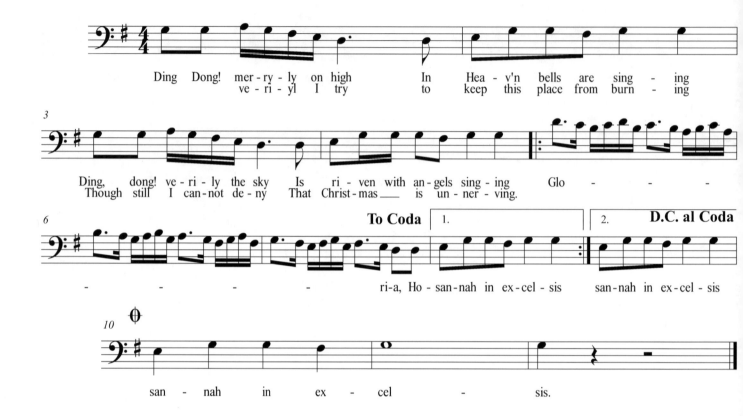

Ding Dong! mer-ry-ly on high   In   Hea-v'n bells are sing - ing
ve-ri-yl I try   to   keep this place from burn - ing

Ding, dong! ve-ri-ly the sky Is ri-ven with an-gels sing-ing Glo - - -
Though still I can-not de-ny That Christ-mas___ is un-ner-ving.

To Coda   1.   2.   **D.C. al Coda**

- - - - ri-a, Ho - san-nah in ex-cel - sis   san-nah in ex-cel - sis

san - nah   in   ex - cel - sis.

Cello

12. Go Tell It On the Mountain

Transcription by Willy Espinoza

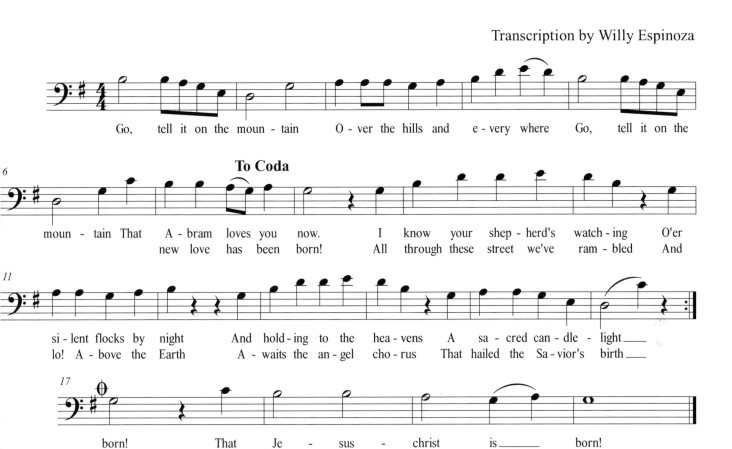

13. God Rest Ye Merry, Gentlemen

Traditional

Arrangement & Transcription by Willy Espinoza

14. Good King Wenceslas

John Mason Neale

Arrangement & Transcription by Willy Espinoza

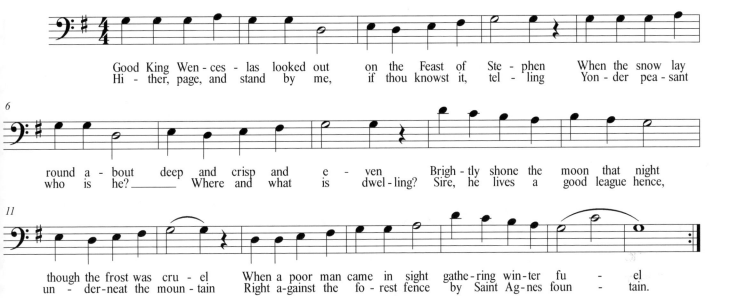

Good King Wen - ces - las looked out on the Feast of Ste - phen When the snow lay
Hi - ther, page, and stand by me, if thou knowst it, tel - ling Yon - der pea - sant

round a - bout deep and crisp and e - ven Brigh - tly shone the moon that night
who is he?_____ Where and what is dwel - ling? Sire, he lives a good league hence,

though the frost was cru - el When a poor man came in sight gathe - ring win - ter fu - el
un - der - neat the moun - tain Right a - gainst the fo - rest fence by Saint Ag - nes foun - tain.

14

15. Hark! The Herald Angel Sings

Music adapted from: "Festgesang" by Felix Mendelssohn,
Arrangement & Transcription by Willy Espinoza

16. I Heard the Bells on Christmas Day

Traditional

Arrangement & Transcription by Willy Espinoza

I heard the bells on Christ - mas day Their old fa - mi - liar ca - rols play And
And in des - pair I bowed my head "There is no peace on Earth," I said For

mild and sweet their songs re - peat Of peace on Earth, good will to men.
hate is strong and mocks the song

17. I Saw Three Ships

The Chieftains

Arrangement & Transcription by Willy Espinoza

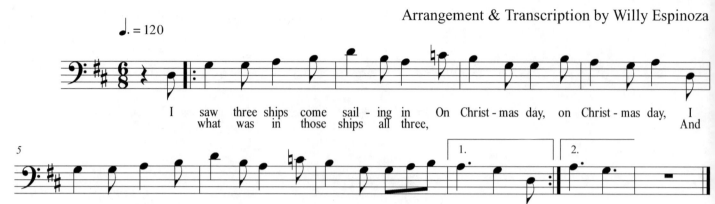

I saw three ships come sail - ing in On Christ - mas day, on Christ - mas day, I
what was in those ships all three,

saw three ships come sail - ing in On Christ - mas day in the mor - ning? And mor - ning.
what was in those ships all three,

17

18. In the Bleak Midwinter

Traditional
Arrangement & Transcription by Willy Espinoza

In the bleak mid-win - ter   Frosty wind made moan   Earth stood hard as i - ron   Wa-ter like a stone

Snow had fal-len Snow   on   Snow __ on snow.   In the bleak mid-win - ter   Long, long a - go.

19. It Came Upon the Midnight Clear

Traditional
Arrangement & Transcription by Willy Espinoza

It came u - pon_ a mid - night clear That glo - rious song_ of old.

From an - gels bend - ding near the earth to touch their harps of gold. Peace

on the earth, good will to men From hea - ven's all gra - cious King The world in

so - lemn still - ness lay To hear the an - gels sing.

20. Jingle Bells

Traditional

Arrangement & Transcription by Willy Espinoza

Jin-gle bells, jin-gle bells jin-gle all the way, Oh what fun it is to ride in a one-horse o-pen

sleigh, hey! one-horse o-pen sleigh! Dash-ing through the snow in a one-horse o-pen sleigh,

O'er the fielda we go, laugh-ing all the way Bells on bob-tails ring, Ma-king spi-rits bright. What

fun it is to ride and sing a sleigh - in song to - night, oh!

21. Jolly Old St. Nicholas

Traditional

Arrangement & Transcription by Willy Espinoza

Jol - ly old St. Ni - cho - las   Lean your ear this way   Don't you tell a   sin - gle soul
Christ-mas Eve is com - ing soon   Now, you dear old man   Whis - per what you'll bring to me

4

1. Whay I'm going to say

2. Tell me if you can.

21

22. Joy to the World

Isaac Watts

Arrangement & Transcription by Willy Espinoza

Joy to the world, the Lord is come Let Earth re-ceive her King. Let e - very heart __ pre-

pare Him room __ And Hea-ven and na - ture sing   And   hea-ven and   na - ture   sing   And

Hea   -   ven,   and   Hea   -   ven,   and   na   -   ture   sing.

23. Il Est Ne

Traditional

Transcription by Willy Espinoza

24. O Christmas Tree

Arrangement & Transcription by Willy Espinoza

O   Christ-mas Tree, O   Christ-mas Tree, How faith-ful are thy bran-ches! O   Christ-mas Tree, O

Christ-mas Tree, How faith-ful are thy bran-ches! Green nos a-lone   in sum-mer-time, But   in the win-ter's

frost and rime;   O   Christ-mas Tree   O   Christ-mas Tree, How   faith-ful are   they   bran-ches.

25. O Come All Ye Faithful

Traditional

Transcription by Willy Espinoza

O   Come   All   Ye   Faith - ful   Joy - ful and trium - phant, O   Come   ye,   O
Sing   choirs of   an - gels,   Sing   in   ex - al - ta - tion___   Sing   all   ye

come___ ye   to   Be - thle - hem.   Come   and   be - hold   Him   Born the Kings of
ci - ti - zens of   hea - ven   a - bove.   Glo - ry   to   God,___   glo - ry   in   the

An - gels; O   come, let   us   a - dore   Him, O   come, let   us   a - dore   Him O   come, let   us   a -
high - est;

dore   Him,_____   Christ,_____   the   Lord.

26. O Come, Little Children

Suzuki

Arrangement & Trascription by Willy Espinoza

27. O Come, O Come, Emmanuel

Arrangement & Transcription by Willy Espinoza

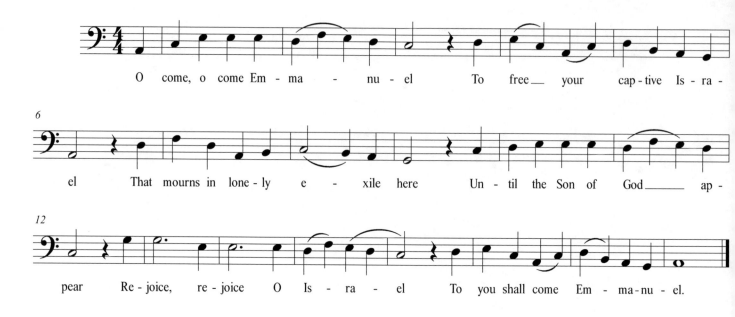

O come, o come Em - ma - nu - el   To free___ your   cap - tive   Is - ra -

el   That mourns in lone - ly   e - xile here   Un - til the Son of God_____ ap -

pear   Re - joice,   re - joice   O Is - ra - el   To you shall come   Em - ma - nu - el.

28. O Holy Night

Adolphe Adam

Arrangement & Transcription by Willy Espinoza

29. O Little Town of Bethlehem

Phillips Brooks (1868)

Arrangemen & Transcription by Willy Espinoza

O lit - tle town of Beth - le - hem How still we see thee lie A bove thy deep and

dream-less sleep The si - lence stars go by Yet___ in thy dark streets shin - eth An e - ver - las - ting

Light The hopes and fears of all these years Are met in thee to - night. si - len - tly, how

si - len - tly The won - drous Goft is given As God im - parts to hu - man hearts The bles - sings of his

Hea - ven Let an - gels sing on Be - thle - hem And let them shine for me. The spi - rit starts with -

in our hearts To fos - ter cha - ri - ty The bles-sing and the bur - den Of sis - ters meek and

well Will come to us, a - bide with us As home we bid fare - well.

30. Once in Royal David's City

Arrangament & Transcription by Willy Espinoza

Once in ro - yal Da - vid's ci - ty Stood a low - ly cat - tle__ shed There a
He came down to earth from hea - ven Who is Gos and Lord of__ all And His

mo - ther laid her ba - by In a man - ger for His bed Ma - ry was a mo - ther
shel - ter was a__ sta - ble And His crad - le was a__ stall With the poor, op-pressed and

mil - ly Je - sus Christ her lit - tle child.
whol - ly Lived on earth our Sa - vior ho - ly

31. Pat-a-Pan

Julie Andrews

Arrangement & Transcription by Willy Espinoza

Wil - lie, bring your lit - tle drum; Ro - bin, bring your   fife and   come; And be   mer - ry while you

play tu-re-lu-re - lu pat-a-pan-a - pan, Come be mer-ry while you play, Let us make our Christ-mas   day!

32. Silent Night

Franz Xaver Gruber

Arrangement & Transcription by Willy Espinoza

Si - lent night, ho - ly night! All is calm, all is bright!

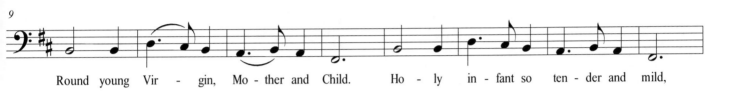

Round young Vir - gin, Mo - ther and Child. Ho - ly in - fant so ten - der and mild,

Sleep in hea - ven - ly peace,_____ Sleep - in hea - ven - ly peace.

33. The First Noel

The first___ No - el, the An - gels did say Was to cer - tain poor
fields___ where they lay keep - ing their sheep On a coold win - ters'

she - pherds in fields as the lay In___
night___ in that was___ so deep.

34. The Friendly Beasts

Traditional

Arrangement & Transcription by Willy Espinoza

Je - sus our bro-ther, strong and good   Was humb-ly   born   in a sta - ble

rude And the friend-ly   beasts a - round his   stood   Je - sus our   bro - ther,   strong and good.

35. The Holly and the Ivy

Traditional

Arrangement & Transcription by Willy Espinoza

The hol-ly and the I - vy, When they both full grown, Of_ all the trees that are

in the wood The_____ hol - ly bears the crown.

36. Up on the Housetop

Benjamin Hanby

Arrangement & Transcription by Willy Espinoza

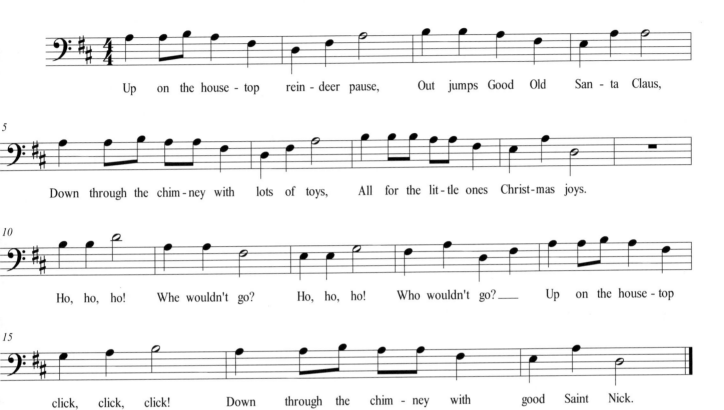

Up on the house - top rein - deer pause, Out jumps Good Old San - ta Claus,

Down through the chim - ney with lots of toys, All for the lit - tle ones Christ-mas joys.

Ho, ho, ho! Whe wouldn't go? Ho, ho, ho! Who wouldn't go?___ Up on the house - top

click, click, click! Down through the chim - ney with good Saint Nick.

37. We Three Kings Of Orient Are

Traditional

Arrangement & Transcription by Willy Espinoza

We three kings of o - ri - ent are Bear - ing gifts we tra - vers a - far Field and foun - tain

Moor and moun - tain Fol - lo - wing yon - der star O___ star of won - der, star of night Star with ro - yal

beau - ty bright West - ward lea - ding, still pro - cee - ding Guide us to thy per - fect light.

38. We Wish You a Merry Christmas

Traditional

Arrangement & Transcription by Willy Espinoza

We wish you a mer-ry Christ-mas we wish you a mer-ry Christ-mas we wish you a mer-ry

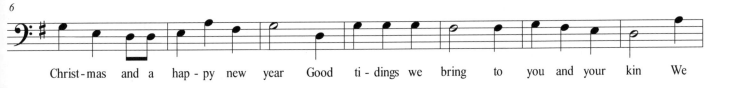

Christ-mas and a hap-py new year Good ti-dings we bring to you and your kin We

wish you a mer-ry Christ-mas and a hap-py new year!

39. What Child Is This?

Traditional

Arrangement & Transcription by Willy Espinoza

What child is this ___ who, laid to rest ___ on Ma - ry's lap, ___ is sleep -

ing? Whom An - gels greet ___ with an - thems sweet ___ while shep - herds watch are keep -

ing? This, this ___ is Christ the King ___ Who shep - herds guards and an - gels sing

Haste, haste ___ to bring him Lord ___ The Babe, ___ the Son ___ of Ma - ry.

40. While Shepherds Watched Their Flocks

Arrangement & Transcription by Willy Espinoza

While shep - herds watched their flocks by night All sea - ted on the ground The
not", said he, for migh - ty dread Had seized their trou - bled mind "Glad

an - gel of the Lords came down And glo - ry shone a - round. "Fear
ti - dings of great joy I bring To you and all man - kind"

41. Rudolph The Red Nosed Reindeer.

Traditional
Arrangement & Transcription by Willy Espinoza

Ru-dolph the Red-Nosed reain-derr,   Had a ve-ry shi-ny   nose,   And if you e-ver

saw   it   you would e-ven say   it   glows   All of   the o-ther   rein-deer,

Ased to laugh and call him   name,   They ne-ver let poos Ru-dolph,   Join in a-ny reain-deer

games.   The one fog-gy Christ-mas Eve,   San-ta came to   say: "Ru-dolph with your

nose so bright,   Won't you guide my   sleigh to-night?"   The how   the rein-deer   loved him.

as they shout-ed out with glee: "Ru-dolph the Red-Nosed Rein-deer,   You'll go down in his-to-ry."

42. Carol of the Bells

Traditional
Arrangement & Transcription by Willy Espinoza

Hark! How the bells Sweet sil-ver bells   All seem to say, "Throw care a-way" Christ-mas is here

Bring - ing good cheer   To young and old   meek and the bold   Ding, dong, ding, dog   That is their song

With joy-ful ring   All ca-ro-ling   Ones seems to hear Words of good cheer From ev'-ry-where   Fil-ling the air

Oh how they pound,   Rai - sing the sound,   O'er hill and dale,   Tel - ling their tale,   Gai - ly they ring

While peo-ple sing   Songs of good cheer Christ-mas is here   mer - ry, mer - ry, mery-ry   mer-ry Christ - mas

mer - ry, mer - ry, mery-ry   mer - ry Christ - mas   Hark! How the bells   Sweet sil - ver bells   All seem to say,

"Throw   care   a - way"

43. Little Drummer Boy

Traditional
Arrangement & Transcription by Willy Espinoza

44. Sing We Now of Christmas

Transcription by Willy Espinoza

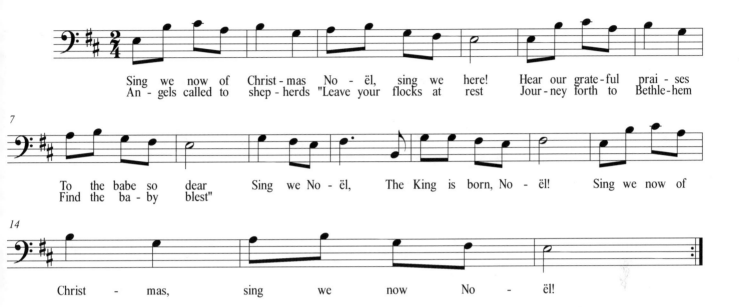

Sing we now of Christ - mas No - ël, sing we here! Hear our grate-ful prai - ses
An - gels called to shep - herds "Leave your flocks at rest Jour - ney forth to Bethle-hem

To the babe so dear Sing we No - ël, The King is born, No - ël! Sing we now of
Find the ba - by blest"

Christ - mas, sing we now No - ël!

45. The Seven Joys Of Mary

Traditional
Arrangement & Transcription by Willy Espinoza

The first good job that Ma - ry had, it was the joy of one. To see her own son,

Je - sus Christ. when he was first her son. When he was first her son, good man, and bless - ed may he

be _____ Oh _____ Fa - ther, Son and Ho - ly Ghost for all e - ter - ni - ty.

46. Alle Jahre Wieder

Traditional
Arrangement & Transcription by Willy Espinoza

E - very sin - gle ye - ar Ba - by - Christ come a - gain.

Down — to the Earth _____ Where all — peo - ple are.

47. Twelve days of Christmas

Arrangement & Transcription by Willy Espinoza

On the first day of Christ-mas my true love sent to me   A part-ridge in a pear tree.   On the

se-cond day of Christ - mas my   true love sent to me   Two tur-tle-doves and a   part-ridge in a pear

tree.   On the third   day of Christ - mas my   true love sent to me   Three   French hens

Two   tur - tle - doves   and   a   part - ridge ___ in a pear   tree.

48. Let it Snow

Frank Sinatraa

Arrangement & Transcription by Willy Espinoza

Oh, the wea-ther out - side is fright - ful but the fire is so de - light - ful. And

since we've no place to go Let it snow, let it snow, let it snow.

49. Ich Steh an Deiner Krippen Hie

ohann Sebastian Bach

Arrangement & Transcription by Willy Espinoza

I stand be - fore Thy man - ger fair, My Je - sus, Life from Hea - ven I

come, and un - to Thee I bear What Thou to me hast gi - ven. Re - ceive it, for 'tis

mind and soul, Heart, spi - rit, strength re - cieve it all And deing to let__ it__ please Thee.

50. Maria durch ein' Dornwald ging

Traditional

Arrangement & Transcription by Willy Espinoza

Ma - ri - a durch ein Dorn-wald ging   Ky - ri-e e-lei - son   Ma - ri - a durch ein

Dorn - wald ging Der   hat   in sie-ben Jahr'n kein Laub   ge-tra-gen   Je - sus und Ma - ri - a.

51. I'm a Little Star

Traditional

Arrangement & Transcription by Willy Espinoza

I'm a lit - tle star,   hang-ing on a tree   See the li - tle chil - dres   dance a-round me
I'm a can-dy stick
I'm a pret-ty an - gel

tra - la - la   tra - la - la   tra - la - la   tra - la - la   tra - la - la   tra - la - la   tra - la - la   la.

52. In France they have Pere Noel

Arrangement & Transcription by Willy Espinoza

In France they have   Pé-re No-ël   In   I - ta-ly, Be - fa - na, In Ger -ma-ny, Kris Krin - gle and

we   know him   as   San - ta Claus.   So ride your sleigh,   sleigh,   sleigh,   let dear

Ru - dolph lead the way so ride your sleigh, sleigh, sleigh   let dear   Ru - dolph lead the way! So ride your

sleigh,   sleigh,   sleigh,   let dear   Ru - dolph lead the way! Up   on   the   roof - tops   high!

53. Ring Rinn Ring The Bells

Traditional

Arrangement & Transcription by Willy Espinoza

Ring, ring, ring the bells, Ring them loud and clear To tell the chil - dren e - very-where That

Christ - mas time is here Ring, ring, ring the bells, Ring them loud and clear To

tell the chil - dren e - very-where That Christ - mas time is here

54. Long time ago on Bethlehem

Traditional

Arrangement & Transcription by Willy Espinoza

Long time a-go in Beth-le-hem, so the Ho-ly bi-ble say   Ma-rys boy child

Je - sus Christ   was   born   on   Christ-mas   day.   Hark now hear   the   an- gels sing   a

King was born   to - day   And man will live for   e - ver more   Be - cause of Christ-mas   day!

55. Frosty the Snowman

Traditional
Arrangement & Transcription by Willy Espinoza

56. Christmas in the old man's hat

Traditional
Arrangement & Transcription by Willy Espinoza

Christ-mas is com-ming and the goose is ge-ting fat   Hey put a pen-ny in the old man's hat!

Light up the fire, ___ the wind is blow-ing cold   San-ta Claus is get-ting old!   Oh

mom-my dear on Christ-mas Day, a-gain I must com-plain   I won-der is it

San-ta Claus who makes mis-takes a-gain   You see there's lit-tle Jen-ny Brown who

got so ma-ny thing___   Dolls and sweets and ted-dy bears and clothes and gol-den rings.

57. I Want a Hippopotamus for Christmas

Traditional

Arrangement & Transcription by Willy Espinoza

58. Santa Claus is Comming To Town

Traditional
Arrangement & Transcription by Willy Espinoza

You bet - ter watch out you bet - ter not cry You bet - ter not pout I'm
ma - king a list He's check - ing it twice He's gon - na find out Who's

tel - ling you why San - ta Claus is com - ming' to town. He's
naugh - ty or nice He

sees you when you're sleep - ing He knows when you're a - wake He know if you've been

bad or good So be good for good - ness sakes

59. Here Comes Santa Claus

Traditional

Arrangement & Transcription by Willy Espinoza

Presto

Here comes San - ta Claus Here comes San - ta Claus right down San - ta Claus Lane

Vi - xcen and Blit - zen and all his rein - ders pul - lin on the reins Bells are ring - ing

chil - dren sing - ing, all is mer - ry and bright So hag your stock - ing and say your pra - yers, 'cause

San - ta Claus comes to - night.

60. It's the Most Wonderful Time of the Year

Andy Williams

Arrangement & Transcription by Willy Espinoza

Prestissimo

It's the most won-der-ful time_____ of the year_____ With the
It's the hap - hap-pi - est sea - son of all_____ With those

kids jin - gle bell - ing, and ev - ry' - one tell - ing you, "Be of good cheer."_____
hol - li - day greet - ings, and gay hap - py meet - ings when friends come to call_____

It's the most won-der-ful time_____ of the year._____
It's the hap - hap-pi - est sea - son of all!

Made in the USA
Columbia, SC
04 December 2024

48450334R00035